D1290316

Be____y

Also by Elise Paschen

POETRY
Houses: Coasts
Infidelities

CO-EDITOR
Poetry in Motion
Poetry in Motion from Coast to Coast
Poetry Speaks
Poetry Speaks Expanded

EDITOR
Poetry Speaks to Children

Bestiary

poems

Elise Paschen

RED HEN PRESS | *Los Angeles, California*

Bestiary

Book design by Jeff Takaki
Author photo by Jennifer Girard

ISBN: 978-1-59709-131-2
Library of Congress Catalog Card Number: 2008929840

The California Arts Council and the National Endowment for the Arts partially
support Red Hen Press.

Published by Red Hen Press
www.redhen.org

First Edition

For Stuart Brainerd
and our children
Alexandra and Stephen

Contents

Bestiary

I think I could turn and live awhile with the animals. . . .

Walt Whitman

I

Monarch

From milkweed to lupine a woman shadows
a monarch. Slowly makes her way, conveys

her weight with care. Inside the womb her son
flutters, then butterfly-kicks against walls.

The woman tracks a trail of burnished wings,
migrating into the heart-notch of forest,

then settles on a lichened tree-trunk where
underground rivers flowing out of snow-

mountain lakes rumble the decree of her
unborn son: *"Journey farther, journey deeper."*

Into darker woods she transports a monarch
ruling, even now, unnamed territory.

Engagement

The king is murdered and his daughter, Mis,
goes mad, growing fur and killer claws, escaping
into the woods. She is tamed by Dubh Ruis, a
harp player. Marrying her, he becomes king.

—Irish legend

Don't touch me, don't come near. I'll shred
your flesh from bone. Don't even stare.

I can smell you from here. You don't
reek like the hunters who tailed me,

all salt and sod. You smack of hay.
Show me what you're hiding. The strings

trap a sun's glint. Sounds like leaf-banter
at night beneath a tree. Here's where

I lay me down – inside this notch.
Strum it for me and let me play.

⚉

What's in your mouth? You take long bites.
It's coming back. A waking whiff—

out on the flagstones in the courtyard,
through the doorways, the grates.

I feel I'm coming home. It's like
a hearth. I never get enough.

꙰

Nights I still rave. The beast is out.
Your arms around me pin it down.

⑥

Your collar's tight. But look. My fingers
have grown shells now, not claws. Stop tying

that cloth across my skin. I need
the air, these woods. Keep here. Let's stay

above moss, beneath leaf. Help me
shake down rowans, rub our flesh red.

You've stripped away the fur, and, after
months of those deer-fat baths, I'm bare.

Moving In

Couple: (*Mech.*) pair of equal and parallel forces acting in opposite directions

Matching some mine with yours, are we a pair?
I alphabetize our vast library
while you hang pictures, revealing a flare
for measuring walls. Do our tastes agree?

The basement hoards our secondary lives:
my leather skirts, high heels; your chessboards, mats
for meditation, keyboards, power drives.
Upstairs we share a wedded habitat.

Suddenly we have two of everything:
his-and-hers alarm clocks – mine, battery-run,
beeps several times when it decides to ring.
Yours – electric – flashes red: 8:01.

Two hammers, two flashlights, two pots for tea,
a pair of ironing boards (yours, unused),
plus several teams of cutlery.
Each object, once spotted, seems reproduced.

"All good things come in pairs," the auctioneer,
eyeing my botanical prints, declares.
We keep each set, but store (just for a year)
all duplicates: my chintz couch, your leather chairs.

We're newlyweds and – who's whose better half?—
although we can't agree, we try to share.
Snuggling beneath a wedding photograph,
we now play Hearts instead of Solitaire.

Barn Owl and Moon

Night-fall, we stretch and tumble under rafters,
beneath the moon. Bats' breath against our lips.
The barn owl and the moon.

A scream, a snore, a hiss, a click, a scratch.
Duets of eyes ignite, burn out the night.

Your heart-shaped face, talons, and tawny skin.
My crescent arc – waxing – all marrow, pearl.

Fixed in the sky. A scythe. Afraid to cut.
We hide. This flash might blind and talons strip.

It's dark. A drumbeat of feathers scales up
my spine. Rapt, out-of-breath, we tilt, take wing.

You clasp a shell of skin. I shed more light
tucked between claw and claw. Rise above earth:
the barn owl and the moon.

Fertility

Early spring, we toe the towpath
along the Delaware and Raritan
Canal. Our sneakers fit the holes
hoofed out by mules a hundred years
ago, hauling barges once heavy
with coal along these muddy banks.

Downstream, near the Bridge Tender's House,
a fisherman above a lock
attempts to trawl for shad. The fish
have returned to their natal rivers
to reproduce and die. We stomp
in muck, six-months-married now, growing

older, and hoping to conceive.
It's spawning season and each roe
shad will release into the water
column 400,000 eggs.
A human female will drop one
egg every month in three days' time.

Let us proliferate like slicks,
hairy-back, skipjack, nanny shad,
though they scrounge the mud floor for food,
ignore their young. We head upstream,
retrace the donkey's labor, towing
the cargo of our hoped-for load.

Trapeze

Sky-bound in someone's yard,
bluebells poke out of dirt.

From back-alley I swing
open our gate to garden.

Beneath the skin your fist
punches: harbinger bud.

A shoot sprouts after snow—
you practice somersaults—

and autumn bulbs now show:
hyacinth, snowdrop, crocus.

How much space will you need
to grow? A galaxy

of cells, then the heartbeat.
You nose-dive down. A dove

hoo, hoo, hooing. Above
lodestar, a slip of moon.

Birth

Armored in red, her voice commands
every corner. Bells gong on squares,
in steeples, answering the prayers.
Bright tulips crown the boulevards.

Pulled from the womb she imitates
that mythic kick from some god's head.
She roars, and we are conquered.
Her legs, set free, combat the air.

Naked warrior: she is our own.
Entire empires are overthrown.

The Flycatcher's Fall

Near the stones marking the Sweat Lodge,
a newborn flycatcher has tumbled
from the nest. "Careful: don't touch it,"
I warn my inquisitive daughter.
"The mother might reject her young."

Perching the flycatcher on bark,
my husband climbs a ladder, slips
the fledgling in a crowded nest.
He teeters, "Not much room up here,"
as beaks open, expecting worms.

Pregnant again, I'm craving something
salty. Our six-month fetus raps
my ribs, demanding food. "The baby
wants her mommy," tugs our daughter
on my sleeve, looking up the tree.

How will this flycatcher sustain
her brood? Will the fallen one starve?
We hear a whistled whit in air
while wing-flutter overhead darkens
the sun. All the small birds respond.

Prey

If my daughter observes the paperback
splayed on the floor beside the barricade

of laundry hampers, wicker baskets, pillows
stuffing the gaps, she will discern I was

the one who hurled the book into the jaws
of 4 a.m., protective of my shrinking

threshold, confounded by feline affection,
attempting to silence the yowling cat

during the hours when sleep escapes, because
his sense of self is fierce, because he cudgels

our bedroom door, because deep down I love
a dog. How throughout each day the cat's paws

battle beneath the study door, how afterwards
he leaps to the armchair beside the desk

green eyes ablaze, long whiskers twitching, striped
fluffed-up tail thumping, full-bellied white heaving.

O Tiger Lily of Pawhuska, orphaned
barn kitten who adopted our young daughter

the day we buried deep my father's ashes:
do not betray my confidence. Don't let

our daughter know I threw the *William Blake*
against the floor to frighten you away,

to stop you clawing into the dark thicket
of night before the birds, your prey, catch fire.

Miss Spider's Guests

"Can the Butterflies come to Miss Spider's Tea Party?"
—International Playthings, Inc.

They swarm Miss Spider's Tea Party: Gnats, June
Beetles, Ladybugs, Flies. The Red Ants stress,
"Don't drop into a cup," meanwhile Moths moon
over bright candles on the cake. "Obsess

about details," instructs Miss Spider. Snake
glides across rug, hissing: "That point is moot.
You trap each guest inside your skein!" "The cake
is honey-sweet," buzz all the Wasps, "A beaut!"

May arrives late, fedora dipped like Garbo,
all feint and mystery. Will Ike now play
his cards, reveal his hand, gent or hobo?
They flutter, feast, and crawl, all night, all day.

Miss Firefly flashes a hefty rhinestone.
Mr. Bumblebee sports too much cologne.

Hive

Tucked in a cleft of arm you hunt
for milk. *Roseate. Areola.*

I circumnavigate the signs
pictured on your pajamas. Arrows

point east and west; a violet hive;
bear: tail-end-up in honey-pot.

Cars drone outside. I comb back tufts
of hair. We burrow in these chintz

pillows, sink deeply down in sofa.
For now, we are a pair spied on

by animals. (A rabbit pokes
its ear, antenna-like, from under

cushions.) I've read "during the summer
honey flow, worker bees will travel

55,000 miles to gather
nectar to make one pound of honey."

A foot kicks off its sock. You sip,
roaming many miles, honey-seeker.

Days tumble. I would like to buzz
into the orchid of your ear.

Sanctuary

[After the War of 1812,] about fifty forts were planned,
stretching from Maine to Louisiana, with Key West being
chosen . . . because of its strategic position near important
shipping lanes.
—*Fort Zachary Taylor State Historic Site* by C.G. Chambers

I

Down past gunrooms, above the ocean swells,
protected by the reef, we track the sun
take its last plunge. I lead you by the hand.
A bagpipe keens across wide-open beach,
while three couples, yards apart, swear and swear.
Beneath the balustrades of the aged fort,
the armament is buried deep – the Parrott
rifles, Rodmans, Columbiads – encased
in sand. The couples on the sand repeat
their lines this New Year's Eve before the sun,
a cannonball, tumbles into the sea.

II

Yellow Fever ravaged the fort in 1862.
Dusk now, new year, mosquitoes swarm. A welt
forms on our daughter's arm. Stepping through ruins
of rock, we spy remains of earlier weddings—
champagne flutes, paper plates, a trail of tulips.
Tracking the march, she scoops up petals, shards

or vows, to carry home. "Would your child eat
a slice of wedding cake?" the caterer asks.
(A cake buried beneath orchids and roses.)
Our three-year-old smiles yes, but as we exit,
I turn to see she's swallowing red blooms.

III

We build our fort. Towering tall, you stretch
the sheet taut, high above our heads. The children
burrow under pillows. Let's keep our vows.
Each night, flashlight in hand, we read aloud
more pages from weathered books. *Blockade-running*
schooners, coasting sea-lanes, never attacked
this harbor. Seeking sanctuary under
the sheets, our brood takes cover while the thunder
discharges like artillery. We sleep
beneath blankets, stone, and mortar, unarmed,
the doors of our houses, unlocked, wide open.

Under Siege

Negotiating this land mine, we scout
more booby traps, seize our stronghold

as he tunnels under chairs, then retreats
when we cut the supply lines and run wires

above ground, blockade all outlets with cushions.
We sweep the vicinity for debris:

a toppled palm, strewn dirt, two cars
flipped over, wriggling fish, and one dead duck.

Raising the blinds to half-mast, we expose
our house to view. By nightfall he is taken,

waves a white cloth. And we, amazed, surrender all.

II

Wi´-gi-e

Anna Kyle Brown. Osage. 1896-1921. Fairfax, Oklahoma.

Because she died where the ravine falls into water.

Because they dragged her down to the creek.

In death, she wore her blue broadcloth skirt.

Though frost blanketed the grass she cooled her feet in the spring.

Because I turned the log with my foot.

Her slippers floated downstream into the dam.

Because, after the thaw, the hunters discovered her body.

Because she lived without our mother.

Because she had inherited headrights for oil beneath the land.

She was carrying his offspring.

The sheriff disguised her death as whiskey poisoning.

Because, when he carved her body up, he saw the bullet hole in her skull.

Because, when she was murdered, the *leg clutchers* bloomed.

But then froze under the weight of frost.

During *Xtha-cka Zhi-ga Tse-the, the Killer of the Flowers Moon.*

I will wade across the river of the blackfish, the otter, the beaver.

I will climb the bank where the willow never dies.

Warning Signs

The sky turns brackish green. I'm caught
outside and hear a rumble growing louder,
stomping the heart. Storm-clouds spit out the grit
of my indecision while I size up

the distance. Before I reach sanctuary
you strike, catch me off balance, then inhale
mortal flesh into air. *Cyclone, whirlwind,*
twister, dust-god. Above the cumulous

I hover. A scrim lifts: the world is radiant.
But you are done. You hurl me down with hail
among the living and the dead. I sprawl
against the dirt. Fish rain from sky.

Afterward

After the downpours, floods, tsunamis, you
lit up the room. The ocean floor erupted.

You blazed that smile. Columns of waves shot back.
Night became day. And then the aftershock

of light. It's black outside since you have dropped
below horizon. I walk past street corners,

now deserted, where once you scorched and burned.
Your god is not my god, so I have suffered

these hand-made sins. The earth revolves. You slide
into the sky unscarred: every ray branding.

Behind the Swan

He claimed no knowledge of that night.
But I could not forget the smack
that bruised and stunned, his appetite,
bill jabs on neck – cannot take back

what he had seized. I tried to reach
the god inside, batter his wings
with words, ignore his barb, his beak.
The beast gropes, guzzles, hovering.

He'll blame the drink, escape behind
the wine, the swan. Feathers inside
my mouth, I remain mute and blind.
A quickening before he flies.

He lives his lie. The bottle rolls.
I ache, cannot stand on the floor.
But my own kind will push to fight:
she'll throw a feast. She'll thrust a knife.

Ghost-Echo

I died.   *You have an out. Again can roam.*

My soul slipped out.   *On walks, you'll notice ankles.*

It walked, then skipped,   *But will you learn to fly,*

Took flight   *Knowing now what they want to hear?*

From here to there,   *Your world will tilt, off-balance.*

Across mountains, a world, *Then you will land*

Landed beyond,   *On firm ground, purchase houses,*

Perched on a sill,   *Time and space out each child,*

Roosted for time   *Make room for generations,*

In your room's rafters.   *Die, reduplicated.*

Disappearing Act

The elsewhere husband doesn't care.
Inside their life, she's on her own,
inhabiting the house, the air.

They share their meal, both unaware,
each one distracted by the phone.
The elsewhere husband doesn't care:

after his work, he climbs the stair,
tumbles with children not yet grown.
She dives through sky, into the air.

Unmoved by the new shade of hair
or those lost pounds, down to the bone,
the elsewhere husband doesn't care.

At the opera how debonair,
the gestures of the baritone.
But no, she smiles, inhales the air.

Why not embark on an affair?
She has the time. She is alone.
The elsewhere husband doesn't care
while she vanishes into air.

Solstice in Snow

Across a month we could not touch;
underground you had slipped, and turned
away, while sky smothered the earth.

The dough needs hands to shape its body.
Our orchard's bare with snow. Inside,
the walls divide, rooms multiply.

I mold the flour throughout the night.
You stomp outside, uprooting snow,
an axe against your shoulder, swearing

to split limbs, branches; trunk from soil.
I trail behind, remind, "Each tree
will overbear its fruit as hands

now drip with dough." No other voice
but yours inside the dark. A stalk
of sun cracks sky. I hear the light

tread of your step as you pronounce
my name, unspoken nights, until
at last we harvest this, our solstice.

Pond in Winter

Throughout the night deliberate steps of mammals
leave an impression upon the sheer sheet

of pond where the Great Blue Heron once dipped
its beak, where the Wood frogs jumped from the hands

of the children, where, in the dead of summer,
a Northern Water snake coiled on the bank,

alive in the sunlight, but now lies buried
beneath the glass. Where do the fish escape,

the minnows, the blue gill? Angels inhabit
the willow trees where Orb Web spiders wove

their evanescent graves. Above the house,
a secret of smoke. The wood burns inside

the grate as it once smoldered under leaves.
From the winter forest a solitary

light rises through a window in thick dusk
as if surfacing, again, out of water.

Sea-Change

We slip under the skin
of ocean, slide into
the brine, float belly-down.

A Barracuda scours.
Gold dangles: fishing lures.
Blue Tang scuttle in sync.

Further below a Tarpon,
lengthy as any man,
cruises the sand floor. Mothers,

we hover: blue fins wave
while hair ripples, escaping.
Will he doubt our authority?

Dripping, we pull our weight
onto the deck. Bats plunge.
Clouds tinge coral. We raise

our young to know the ocean
heaves every grain. Night falls.
Suspended between timber

and foam, buoyed, then dropped,
we pitch, catch hold. The sea
cradles the sighing hull.

Isthmus

Across the centuries, I navigated
rivers, tributaries, even an ocean

to land upon this bank, secure foothold.
I waited every night for the arrest

of night, until I discovered your limbs
branching against the sky. So I touched bark,

shimmied down trunk, swallowed loose rain off leaves
and cupped this resin in hand; until now

shipwrecked, anchored here, on the prow, I'm netted
to your chest, belly-up, sternum to spine.

Squibnocket

... thence across in a straight line to Squibnocket
pond ... thence across the beach to the sea in a
southwest direction, as marked by stones.
—*The History of Martha's Vineyard*, 1911

Stone walls coil along the hillside.
The ringneck snake, dead near the spring,
hisses while we fill pitchers high
with tumbling water.

After a swim, my husband's mouth
tastes like salt water, and the waves
torpedo the shore, staging war
behind dune trenches.

As for our meal, my husband conjures
an untouchable sky. We place
a table beside the stone wall,
then anchor down

leaves of napkins, arranging china
constellations – *The Little Dipper*,
The Cup, *The Lyre*, tumblers of salt,
pitchers of water.

Rock clouds collide above the pond,
wafer-thin, while the northern harrier,
or marsh hawk, slowly spirals down
to seize its prey.

We'll track her nest by improvising.
Perhaps the weathervane will chart
her flight? The letters scrawled across
the sundial read:

The sun, always the sun, but oftentimes
the moon. The weathervane declares:
"Look to the hawk." The harrier circles
the pond, the hills,

mistaking the meandering wall
of stone for some ancient lost snake,
deliberately aims, banking air,
then dives straight down.

Chancing Upon the Manatees

The journey's tough:
troughs or else shoals
challenge each crossing.
We navigate
the Avenue:
do we change course
or simply sail
the puddle's ocean?
—"Columbus"

Steering children across
the Millennium lawn, we hear drums'
rumble, the sirens' caterwauling
across Columbus, and we spy
remains of the parade: a float
decked with teenage girls, dressed in gowns.
Our three explorers, step in time,
rat-a-tat march, their first Columbus
Day parade.
The year 1493
when Christopher Columbus sighted
three mermaids rising out of ocean,
beyond the coast of Hispaniola.
He noted the discovery
of manatees, West Indian,
from the species *Sirenius*,
lumbering mammals sailors mistook
for sirens waving.
We pilot our crew
away from the parade, seek higher

terrain and climb the bank to Plensa's
fountain. Our daughter, son, and niece
become transfixed, then splash and wade,
squealing as they discover water.
We pull them from the shallows dripping
from the calves down. Our son kicks off
a shoe.

                       Searching for manatees
in Captiva, our daughter lost
her sneaker, running to the harbor's edge
to spot a meandering creature.
Land-bound, we don't confuse the shy
ponderous sea-cow for a siren.
A shadow navigates between
motorboats, a mistaken mermaid,
on the brink of vanishing from sight.

Raccoon on a Branch

You want to face this illness on your own.
I take a plane to be near. Your physique,
still handsome, racked by coughs, by monthly chemo.

It's difficult for you to speak. I'm tongue-tied.
As I leave, walking down your block, ground trembles.
I meet another friend recovering.

She and I follow the reservoir path.
We've walked this trail before. Though you're not here,
you occupy the space that separates.

I tell my friend you want to be alone.
She says, "That's strange. After the operation,
I needed to be near all those I love."

We hear a scuffling in some fallen branches
scattered across the dirt. Crows caw above.
My friend stops, gestures: "Look, a young raccoon."

The creature stares straight at us. A dog barks.
The animal limps away, climbs a trunk.
He fumbles, ascends to a higher branch,

looks down, trembling, unfocused, blinks his eyes,
unaccustomed to the blazing sun. Leaving
behind the raccoon, clinging close to limb,

we understand he wants no company.
The light is changing now, but I'd stay planted
beneath the tree, waiting into the dark.

III

The Broken Swan

When my mother's body is seized with uncontrollable
twitching, she begins to reminisce about dancing in Venice.

When the soft-spoken nurse with the long black braid positions her head
for the EEG, my mother quips she is *finally having her hair done.*

My mother begins talking about Japan, how they would pray,
kneeling on *tatami* mats, how the Japanese were her most devoted fans.

She explains to all of us, gathered around her hospital bed,
the nurses, the residents, the interns, the neurologist,

about raw fish, as if we have never before heard of *sushi*
or *sashimi,* and she chats about *sake,* as if it were 1958

again, and how her partner, André Eglevsky, drank *sake*
before *Swan Lake,* and, during a *corsage* lift, let her drop.

Then she describes the gondoliers in their barges,
waiting on the canals. How, when my father arrived

at the Gritti Palace dressed in worn-down jeans,
she worried *the concierge would turn us away.*

I catch a glimpse of my mother, the woman I had seen
last week on PBS, during a seventies interview, older

than I am now, but looking years younger, wearing
blue eye shadow, saying, *if I am able to be beautiful and graceful*

or regal or dramatic, then I have accomplished
what I set out to do as a ballet dancer. In the hospital

I witness the mother I had known in all her imperial
elegance, who practices the phrases she once had taught,

saying, "thank you, love" and "how are you, angel?"
and "are you comfortable?" Not the woman she has become

since my father died: every day wearing the same black tee shirt,
demanding, "Where are my pills?" or "Turn on the TV!"

Under the glare of fluorescent lights, my mother arches
her neck, as if on stage, feathering before her rapt audience.

Ash

"There's a moth trapped inside the fire,"
my daughter says, but I explain,
"No, it's an ash." She asks, "Like Paba?"

A month before, we had transported
my father's ashes on a plane
to Oklahoma. When we boarded,

Airport Security insisted
on viewing my father's remains
inside the urn. After they pried

the lid, the crack kept fissuring.
The day before my father died,
a tree surgeon hacked down the ash

which towered tall above our house.
Struck by lightning, the tree had split
in two, about to strike the roof.

My father, cut down by disease,
could no longer swallow or speak,
yet he wanted to sit upright

in his cane-back chair. I knelt on
the oak floor, holding his gnarled hands.
We shuddered to hear the buzz saw

chop down the branches. Early June.
Outside my father's house, the wood
shavings hovered in air like moths.

Crossing

After your departure, the halls
stretched even farther, miles of marble.

The women whispered as if death
knew no one's name, forgetting I

stood there, stone-still, a water pitcher
offered to you. Your thirst was not

easily quenched. Their voices offered
small comfort, insisting this passage

would last into eternity.
Before the ceremony, after

the baths, my mother fastened pearls,
your wedding gift, around my neck

with hands that knew their chore as if
repeated, daughter after daughter.

Later, nothing could take more time.

Eurydice

In 1947, I told [Stravinsky] that I would like to
do a new, modern *Orpheus*. It seemed to me that
the Orpheus myth, with its powerful portrayal
of the poet-musician's destiny and of his love, was
particularly appropriate for ballet....
                                    —George Balanchine

My mother, twenty-three, is married
to Balanchine. The nights he spends,
absorbed, at work on *Orpheus*
she feels alone, and stays at home,
stitching an Indian-patterned skirt.
But when she dances Eurydice's

last pas de deux, she wraps her arms
and legs around her poet husband,
Orpheus, willing him to look
into her eyes. As Balanchine
writes: "tormented because she cannot
be seen by the man she loves."

Attempting to seduce, she begs
him with her dance until he tears
away his mask. Then she sinks down
to earth and dies. During rehearsal
Stravinsky asks, "How long to die?"
In the score he scratches five counts.

The time of the ballet, "the time
of sand and snakes, of Greek earth legends"
writes Balanchine. And Kirstein
(describing their Gluck's *Orpheus*):
"the eternal domestic tragedy
between an artist and his wife."

Her husband, armed with song, lays siege,
enchants the gods to claim her back,
vowing he will not look. But she
persuades him. Therefore Orpheus
throws off his mask, and loses her.
His mask becomes a lyre.

Mother, when I was young, I watched
you from the wings and saw the sweat
dripping from arms and neck, your gasp
for breath. I thought it was your last.
But no. You'd towel off, and then
step back into the spotlight, smiling.

Mary of Magdala

Mary called Magdalene, out of whom went seven devils.

—*Luke 8.2*

They jibe and poke, squeeze behind doors,
under floorboards, twittering and jeering.

Look there: see them? The ink well spills.
A chair falls. Latch windows. Bolt doors.

I hide inside this house, my cave,
avoid the eyes of strangers. I'm

buried inside. *But then an earthquake*
rolls back the stone: lets in the light.

He stands alone. His words, like fish,
swim through my bones. So I will follow.

But after transporting the jars
of aloes, myrrh, down to the sepulcher,

no one believes: "She is a woman,
Mary of Magdala, and mad."

Inside the tomb, my tears turn earth
to mud. And shining ones inquire:

Why seek the living among the dead?
Under almond branches, I'm blinded

by sun. A man in gardener's clothes
utters my name. "Do not touch me."

Where you seek permanence is death.
Where you seek change, there you find life.

I kneel inside the tomb. *As if an earthquake
rolls back the stone: lets in the light.*

Outside the Tomb

Uproar of finch in olive leaves.
The angels spoke,

but I was blind. A gardener called.
If only pores

could drip with honey, bones would shine.
Let me explore

tuber and truss, tunic and whorl,
serve as your sole

translator: *miniature star, sun,*
dazzler, just wings.

You spoke my name, I understood.
Before I leave

this garden, climb clay path,
mountains of rock,

before I speak in parables,
appear again.

Farewell

For Sam, the dog

Still there is light, and stands of trees,
though nettles cut, and sun may burn,
though you are gone deep in the earth,
still grass, still wings, still there are trees.

Though you are gone deep in the earth—
I dig the dirt, I dig the dirt—
it's caught beneath my nails, the dirt,
deep in the earth. And you are gone.

Out on the road, under the sun,
though nettles cut and then will burn,
you're in the grass, you are the sun.
We share the light. Forget the night.

But let me breathe. Are you in air?
I smell the dirt. The earth is still.
I walk the road: you are not there.
The night comes down. I breathe in still.

Under the Dome

At times they will fly under. The dome
contains jungles. Invent a sky under the dome.

Creatures awake, asleep, at play, aglow:
they float – unbottled genii – under the dome.

Southern Belle, a splash of black, dusted with gold,
dissembles, *assembling*, acts shy under the dome.

Cattleheart, Giant Swallowtail, Clipper:
sail, navigate sky high under the dome.

Like confetti – a wedding – bits of Rice
Paper: sheer mimicry under the dome.

Magnificent Owl, in air, a pansy,
it feeds, wings up, eye to eye, under the dome.

Name them: Monarch, then Queen, last Viceroy.
What will scientists deify under the dome?

Basking against a leaf: a Banded Orange,
displayed like a bowtie under the dome.

A living museum. Exist to be observed:
never migrate, but live, then die, under the dome.

Lips, lashes, eyes. From the outside in,
do beings magnify under the dome?

Lepidoptera. From the Greek: *scale-wing.*
Chrysalis. Stay, butterfly, under the dome.

Cicadas

Forty years ago this night (a whir now
with the cicadas' never-dying thrum)
inside the rambling family beach house,
you slept, the stone sleep of an eight-year-old,
until the sirens wrenched the house awake.

Years ago, trains freighted cattle in cars
headed to the Chicago slaughter yards,
but your Uncle Charles, a meat-packing heir
and bachelor, who owned this once-estate,
stabled his Jersey cows behind blue-tinted

glass, providing milk for his weekend guests.
Our rented house, built on the site of grass
tennis courts, remains flanked by aging sycamore,
hemlock. A map displays the summer gardens,
Rabbitry and Ornamental Bird Pond.

That night your mother had declined the offer,
made by a friend, to take the children out
for ice cream treats. Instead, she tucked each child
safely in bed. The crash of waves lulled you
to sleep, but then you heard the sirens racing

down Red Arrow Highway. The speeding pickup,
chased by a police car, killed instantly
the young mother and her two children
crossing the road for ice cream. Their car radio
drowned out the police car's alarm.

We search for sleep, but the crescendo
of the cicadas, clustered in the leaves,
swells and distends, a train that never reaches
its destination. An Amtrak train blasts
its horn while the cicadas clatter on.

Cradle-Song

As she sleeps the retriever barks
at the back door. A frying pan
clangs against floor. Upon the island
father splits carrots into diamonds.

As she sleeps the computer hums
while a train bellows down the sky.
Every dusky star flares alone.
Overhead a plane thunders by.

As she sleeps the oak floorboards creak.
Across the rug, a sprig of light.
She navigates the galaxies—
the moon, her quilt. Let down the night.

Threshold

My father is dying. I cannot breathe.
He is leaving home, and I now must try
to close the door and lock it with his key.

He no longer inhabits the moth-wing
pages from the book of childhood, but travels
beyond the door, inside the past, concealed

behind the rack of clothes, the story's attic,
the place he would describe before I fell
asleep. The book lies open on the pillow.

I shut my eyes, try to count stars or stairs
climbing always beyond reach. It's too soon
for him to leave. I still must learn to place

one foot before the other and to wake
the words from sleeping letters, so I wait
for him to read the book. When day turns dark,

the key revolves, and he, with bear-tight arms,
catches me all in air — I ride his shoe
across the wood to the unending hall.

Feast for the Living

I dream my father is alive, preparing
the Ocean Drive house for a dinner party.
Together we walk down the aisles, my father

steering the cart, selecting favorite foods:
dark chocolate, crisp baguettes, smoked salmon,
buttery Chardonnay, chickens, romaine.

At home, he clips basil and thyme from garden,
pulls on his chef's apron and improvises,
reigning over the stove. Throughout our dinners

he would declare, "Let the wine flow," and we,
his family and friends, would travel down
a garnet river, bubbling, rippling, clinking

under the wind-blown stars, swapping the stories
of our shared adventures, the tales of places
he had navigated across the globe.

My father shows me how to poach, sauté,
and whisk, as he conjures from scratch this dinner
for his wife, my mother. "What's the occasion?"

I ask. While stirring he explains, to prepare
my mother for his departure,
so she will make new friends, once he is gone.

First Snow

As if released, at last, into light sleep,
the dozing off, the stillness of the earth,
the hush, the fall, surrendering the soul:

first snow transfigures the November woods
with its brush-off, its hide-and-seek, just-born
then-gone. A tree-stand, once shuttered by leaves,

now visible, towers. Two hounds, without
their master, sniff frozen terrain. An antlered
stag hooves cloven tracks: in his wake, a crossbow

of branches. The tumbled trunk. A gunshot
ricochets. The intermission of day.
While trees, dark ghosts beyond the clearing, slumber.

Magnificent Frigatebird

Slapdash of waves. White onyx moon. Sea turtles
crack out of shells beneath the sand while overhead

ocean birds, like ampersands, punctuate
the sky. *Conjoin, conjoin.* They link earthbound

sentences – *How long to walk on this ground?*
How short our stay? – during that man-o'-war

struggle between the dirt and air. *Which part*
to keep? Which part to give away? I celebrate

your birth, stretching out half a century,
while you read outside the sea grass hut, minutes

before the end of day. Perched on the deck,
interrogating the sun, I look up.

Above, a Magnificent Frigatebird
hovers mid-air, his silhouetted shape,

a tilde symbol. Beneath his superscription
we're grounded, transfixed, as if his swung dash

marked this spot on the sand or else transformed
the articulation of every limb.

As if we were some notes on a keyboard
waiting to be altered into a sound

or chord never practiced. I try to read
the horizon. Your voice roots out my name.

Acknowledgments

"Birth" is dedicated to Alexandra Brainerd; "Hive" to Stephen Brainerd; "Sea-Change" to Lisa Lee; "Raccoon on a Branch" to Jason Shinder; "Under the Dome" to Agha Shahid Ali; and "Magnificent Frigatebird" to Stuart Brainerd.

Grateful acknowledgment is made to the editors of the following publications:

Court Green (Dossier: Bouts-Rimés): "Miss Spider's Tea Party"; *Crab Orchard Review*: "Fertility"; *CutThroat*: "Sanctuary," "The Flycatcher's Fall," "*Wi'-gi-e*," "First Snow," and "Magnificent Frigatebird"; *Eclectic Literary Forum*: "Under the Dome" (as "Ghazal") and "Farewell"; *The Hudson Review*: "Squibnocket," "Disappearing Act," and "The Broken Swan"; *The New Republic*: "Monarch" and "Sea-Change"; *The New Yorker:* "Columbus" (epigraph on page 48); *Ploughshares*: "Engagement"; *Shenandoah*: "Barn Owl and Moon" and "Solstice in Snow"; *TriQuarterly*: "Raccoon on a Branch," "Outside the Tomb," "Feast for the Living," and "Warning Signs"; *Valparaiso Poetry Review:* "Cicadas," "Hive," and "Moving In"; *Verb*: audio version of "Trapeze."

The following poems appeared in these anthologies:

"Under the Dome" (as "The Dome") in *Ravishing DisUnities: Real Ghazals in English* (Wesleyan, 2000); "Mary of Magdala" (as "Mary Magdalen") was written to celebrate twenty years of women at Magdalen College, Oxford, and published in *Magdalen College Record 2000*; "Birth Day" in *Birthday Poems: A Celebration* (Thunder's Mouth Press, 2002) and *Poetry 180: A Turning Back to Poetry* (Random House, 2003); "Farewell" in *The Breath of Parted Lips: Voices from the Robert Frost Place*, Volume II (CavanKerry Press, 2004); "Ghost-Echo" in *Chance of a Ghost: An Anthology of Contemporary Ghost Poems* (Helicon Nine Editions, 2005); "Eurydice" (as "Tallchief in Orpheus") in *Tributes: Celebrating Fifty Years of New York City Ballet* (William Morrow, 1998) and *Dance*

Poems (Knopf, Everyman's Library, 2006); "Chancing Upon the Manatees" in *The Dire Elegies: 60 Poets on Endangered Species of North America* (FootHills Publishing, 2006); "Threshold" in *Fatherhood Poems* (Knopf, Everyman's Library, 2007); "Behind the Swan" (as "Leda") in *Conversation Pieces: Poems that Talk to Other Poems* (Knopf, Everyman's Library, 2007); "Engagement" in *Letters to the World* (Red Hen Press, 2008); "Sanctuary" in *Breathe: 101 Contemporary Odes* (C+R Press, 2008); "Birth Day" and "Monarch" in *Poetry Speaks: The Poetry Lover's 2005 Calendar*; "Columbus," "Under Siege," and "Barn Owl and Moon" in *Poetry Speaks: The Poetry Lover's 2006 Calendar*; "Miss Spider's Guests" in *Poetry Speaks: The Poetry Lover's 2007 Calendar*; "Isthmus" in *Poetry Speaks: The Poetry Lover's 2008 Calendar*; "Warning Signs" and "Cradle-Song" in *Poetry Speaks: The Poetry Lover's 2009 Calendar*.

"Pond in Winter," a "winter" poem, written for the Three Oaks Poet Laureateship, was published in *Harbor Country News*, January 3, 2008. "Barn Owl and Moon" was written to accompany "The Barn Owl and the Moon" sculpture by Kathleen Scarboro.

"Wi-gi-e" means "prayer" in Osage. The poem is spoken by Mollie Burkhart, whose sister, Anna Kyle Brown, was murdered during the Osage Reign of Terror (1921—1926) when outsiders married Osage women and then killed them for their headrights. During this period of history, the Osages were considered one of the wealthiest people in the world because of the oil discovered on their land. My own family, the Tallchiefs, lived in Fairfax, Oklahoma during this time.

I would like to express gratitude to the Tyrone Guthrie Centre for a writer's residency and to the Newberry Library for granting me the Frances C. Allen Fellowship to research the Osage Reign of Terror.

I also would like to honor the memory of two beloved friends who supported this work: the poets Agha Shahid Ali and Jason Shinder. Deep gratitude to those who, throughout the years, have encouraged these poems: John Fuller, Frank Bidart, Dana Gioia, Grace Schulman, Molly Peacock, Richard Howard, Susan Hahn, and Joy Harjo. Many thanks, also, to Julie Parson Nesbitt, Michael Warr, De Gray, Lisa Lee, Tree Swenson, and, always, to Cynthia Atkins.

Biographical Note

Elise Paschen is the author of *Infidelities*, winner of the Nicholas Roerich Poetry Prize, and *Houses: Coasts*. Her poems have been published in *The New Republic, Ploughshares,* and *Shenandoah*, among other magazines, and in numerous anthologies. She is editor of the *New York Times* best-selling anthology *Poetry Speaks to Children* and co-editor of *Poetry Speaks, Poetry Speaks Expanded, Poetry in Motion,* and *Poetry in Motion from Coast to Coast*. Former Executive Director of the Poetry Society of America, she is the co-founder of "Poetry in Motion," a nationwide program which places poetry posters in subways and buses. Paschen teaches in the Writing Program at The School of the Art Institute of Chicago.